This book belongs to:

....

....

Dear Fellow Artist,

I'm grateful that you've chosen this adult coloring book as a tool for relaxation, meditation, and calmness of mind. By selecting this book, you've made a decision to invest in your own well-being and prioritize your self-care.

As you immerse yourself in the intricate interior designs within this book, I hope you'll experience the therapeutic benefits of coloring. You'll find a sense of peace, mindfulness, and a release from stress and anxiety.

I'm confident that this coloring book will guide you towards a state of zen, and allow you to reconnect with yourself. May the colors on these pages inspire you to unleash your creativity and find moments of joy and tranquility in your daily life.

Thank you for joining me on this journey towards inner peace and self-care.

With gratitude,

Lolita Diamond
@lolitartwork

With Love

@lolitartwork

ABOUT THE AUTHOR

Lolita Diamond is a passionate advocate for self-care, mindfulness, and creativity. From a young age, she found solace in the act of coloring, and it became a therapeutic tool for her to cope with the challenges of life.

As she grew older, Lolita never lost her love for art and found that it continued to be a powerful tool for relaxation and stress relief. Over the years, she has experimented with different designs, patterns, and colors, and has discovered the endless possibilities of coloring as an art form.

After experiencing the transformative power of coloring firsthand, Lolita was inspired to share this gift with the world. She began creating her own designs and patterns, experimenting with different techniques and styles, and eventually compiled her work into a series of coloring books.

Through her books, Lolita hopes to inspire others to embrace coloring as a tool for self-care, mindfulness, and creativity. She believes that coloring is not just an activity for kids, but a therapeutic tool for people of all ages and backgrounds.

Lolita is also a devoted animal lover and finds great joy in spending time with her furry friends. When she's not making art, you can often find her taking her dog for a walk or cuddling with her cat.

Her ultimate goal is to inspire others to prioritize their self-care and find moments of peace and tranquility in their daily lives. With her coloring books, Lolita hopes to guide others towards a state of calmness, relaxation, and creativity.

Join Lolita Diamond on this journey towards self-discovery and self-care, and unleash your inner artist through the magic of coloring.

Dear Friend,

As you come to the end of this coloring book, I hope that you feel a sense of calmness and rejuvenation. Coloring is more than just an activity - it is a form of therapy that allows you to disconnect from the outside world and connect with your inner self.

Through this book, I hope that I have inspired you to prioritize your self-care and to embrace your creativity. I believe that each and every one of us has an inner artist waiting to be unleashed, and that coloring is a powerful tool to help us tap into that creativity.

Remember that self-care is not selfish - it is essential. Take time for yourself, connect with nature, and always remember to breathe. When we take care of ourselves, we can better show up for the people and the world around us.

I want to thank you for choosing this book and for allowing me to be a part of your journey towards self-discovery and self-care. It has been an honor to share my passion for coloring with you, and I hope that you continue to find joy and peace in this therapeutic practice.

Until we meet again, keep coloring and keep shining your light.

With love and gratitude,

Lolita Diamond
@lolitartwork

If you loved this **book**, I would be forever grateful if you could please take a moment to leave a review on your favorite social media platform. Your feedback will not only help others discover the **magic** of coloring, but it's also really encouraging! It would help me improve my work and continue **to** create content that resonates with you.

Thank you for **choosing** this book and for allowing me to be a part of your journey towards mindfulness and **creativity**. Your support means everything to me, and I can't wait to see what beautiful **creations** you bring to life through the magic of coloring.

LOLITARTWORK

Let's stay in touch
@lolitartwork

Made in United States
Troutdale, OR
12/29/2023

16504168R20060